EXTREME SPORTS BIOGRAPHIES ™

KEVIN JONES
Snowboarding Champion

Ian F. Mahaney

The Rosen Publishing Group's
PowerKids Press™
New York

To my wife, Jenet

Safety gear, including helmets, wrist guards, warm clothing, and protective gloves, should be worn while snowboarding. Do not attempt tricks without proper gear, instruction, and supervision.

Published in 2005 by The Rosen Publishing Group, Inc.
29 East 21st Street, New York, NY 10010

First Edition

Editor: Heidi Leigh Johansen
Book Design: Mike Donnellan
Layout Design: Kim Sonsky
Photo Researcher: Peter Tomlinson

Photo Credits: Cover, pp. 4, 7 (inset), 11, 15, 16, 19, 20 (inset), 22 © Shazamm; p. 7 © Duomo/CORBIS; p. 8 © Gunter Marx Photography/Corbis; p. 8 (inset) © AP/Wide World Photos; p. 12 © Mark Gallup/Icon SMI; p. 20 © Bob Winsett/CORBIS.

Library of Congress Cataloging-in-Publication Data

Mahaney, Ian F.
Kevin Jones : snowboarding champion / Ian F. Mahaney.—1st ed.
    p. cm. — (Extreme sports biographies)
Includes bibliographical references and index.
ISBN 1-4042-2745-8 (Library Binding)
1. Jones, Kevin, 1975—Juvenile literature. 2. Snowboarders—United States–Biography—Juvenile literature. [1. Jones, Kevin, 1975– 2. Snowboarders.] I. Title. II. Series.

GV857.S57M35 2005
796.93'092—dc22

                            2003024202

Manufactured in the United States of America

Contents

Kevin Jones performs a snowboarding trick in which he jumps into the air off an obstacle, bends his knees, and grabs the snowboard with one hand.
Inset: Kevin smiles for the camera before an awards show.

Extreme Snowboarding

Snowboarding is an **extreme sport**. Snowboarders, also called riders or boarders, strap their boots to a **lightweight** wooden board and ride down a snow-covered mountain. There are several types of snowboarding. The most popular type is called freeriding. In freeriding, snowboarders ride down a mountain, often sharing the slopes with **skiers**. Freeriders jump into the air and do tricks off the snowy bumps and curves of the mountain. Another type of snowboarding is called freestyle. In freestyle snowboarding, riders snowboard in a special area of a mountain that has **obstacles**, including **half-pipes**. The riders jump into the air off the obstacles and **perform** tricks in midair. Kevin Jones is one of the best freestyle snowboarders in the world. He is known for his fearless riding and his **amazing** tricks.

Getting to Know Kevin Jones

Kevin Christopher Jones was born in Sacramento, California, on January 23, 1975. Sacramento is the capital of California. Kevin's parents, Peggy and Mitch Jones, Kevin, and his three siblings lived in El Dorado Hills, outside Sacramento. As a child and teenager, Kevin loved to skateboard. When Kevin was 17 years old, he saw a snowboarding movie called *Riders on the Storm*. Kevin became very interested in snowboarding. He tried snowboarding on a nearby mountain called Iron Mountain and fell in love with the sport. To Kevin it felt like skateboarding on snow. From the second he strapped his boots to a snowboard, Kevin knew he was a snowboarder. Kevin often rides with other snowboarders, including Tara Dakides and Shaun White. They ride on many mountains in the United States, including Mammoth Mountain in northern California.

People call snowboarders "shredders" because snowboarders shred, or cut up, the snow when they crisscross the mountain slopes. Inset: Most boarders, including Kevin, shown here, ride a snowboard with their left foot forward.

Shown here is a line of colorful, modern snowboards. Inset: Jake Burton, shown with one of his snowboards, made the first wooden snowboard with a plastic bottom for smooth riding in the 1970s. Before that, snowboards were heavy and hard to control. Burton still makes snowboards today!

The First Snowboards

About 65 years before Kevin Jones started shredding the slopes in California on his lightweight wooden snowboard, people were strapping their boots to pieces of wood and riding down snowy mountains. In the 1960s, a man named Sherman Popper attached two skis together so that his children could ride down a mountain. Popper used **materials** that worked well on snow. He called his invention a snurfer. The word "snurfer" is a combination of the words "snow" and "**surfer**." In the 1970s, snowboarders began riding with one foot positioned in front of the other foot on the snowboard. That made it easier to control the big board on the downhill slopes. Kevin rides the board with his left foot forward. Boarders who ride with their right foot forward are called goofy-footers. When Kevin snowboards, he looks like a surfer on snow!

As a teenager, Kevin Jones picked up snowboarding quickly. He first boarded in 1992, when he was 17 years old. He entered his first **competition** the following year. Because of Kevin's skateboarding past, he was already used to moving quickly while balancing with both feet on a single board. In the beginning, Kevin boarded because it was fun and extreme. He did not know then that one day he would become a **professional**, or pro, snowboarder. Kevin entered more snowboarding competitions and did so well that several snowboarding companies decided to **sponsor** him. This means that these companies gave Kevin snowboarding clothes and gear for free. They also paid for Kevin to enter competitions. Thanks to his hard work and talent, Kevin became a professional snowboarder before he was 20 years old.

Kevin is famous for his boardslides. He performs a boardslide by jumping onto an obstacle, such as a railing or a table, and using his board to slide along the obstacle. Railings and tables are often found in freestyle courses.

Kevin is excellent in the big air and slope style competitions because he is a very creative boarder. He is known for performing amazing tricks in the air. Kevin enjoys other freestyle events, such as riding the half-pipe, but he does not usually compete on the half-pipe in competitions.

The Main Events

In competitions Kevin Jones performs best in two freestyle events. The first event is called the big air competition. In the big air competition, snowboarders ride down a steep **ramp** and jump off the bottom lip of the ramp. They perform **complex** tricks in the air, such as 360-degree spins, before landing on a smooth slope below. One full circle equals 360 degrees.

The second event is called slope style. Slope style is an event in which snowboarders ride down a slope that has obstacles on it, such as railings, jumps, and tables. The snowboarders perform interesting tricks using these obstacles. Kevin has won **medals** in both the big air event and the slope style event at many major snowboarding competitions. Kevin won a silver medal in the slope style event at the 2001 World Snowboarding **Championships**.

The X Games is a competition of extreme sports that is held every year. Skateboarding, wakeboarding, and snowboarding are examples of sports featured at the X Games. Kevin first competed at the Winter X Games in 1997. Between 1997 and 2001, Kevin won nine medals at the Winter X Games. That number of medals is more than any other person has won at the Winter X Games. This makes Kevin one of the most successful Winter X-Games **champions** ever. Two of Kevin's best years at the X Games were 2000 and 2001. He won the gold medal both years in the slope style event. He also took home the 2000 bronze medal in the big air event. In a short period of time, Kevin had become one of the most respected boarders in the world. He was even named Rider of the Year by the popular magazine *Snowboarder* three years in a row!

Kevin holds up his board and shows off the gold medal he won in the slope style event at the 2001 Winter X Games. In second and third place are Todd Richards and Jussi Oksanen.

It takes a lot of skill to be able to perform hard tricks in midair and then to land on a snowy mountain slope. Kevin's ability to make snowboarding tricks look smooth and easy has won him many fans.

Kevin's Cool Moves

Kevin Jones is widely respected in the snowboarding community. He is known for his smooth style of snowboarding. Many people think that Kevin makes hard tricks look easy. One famous trick that Kevin performs is the frontside 900. This trick is extreme! Kevin performs this trick by pushing off the front edge of his snowboard, or the side closest to his toes, and jumping into the air. Then he performs a 900-degree spin, which is spinning two and one-half times in the air. Kevin's smooth landings have earned the trick the nickname "frontside Jones." When a snowboarder spins one-half, one and one-half, or two and one-half times, he or she lands facing in the opposite direction from the starting direction. Facing opposite the starting direction on a snowboard is called riding fakie. Many of the hardest snowboarding tricks require the boarder to land in the fakie position.

Extreme Snowboarding Equipment

Freeride snowboarders and freestyle snowboarders ride different types of snowboards. The front tip of a freeride snowboard is curved to make riding through powdery snow easier. Freestyle snowboards, like the ones that Kevin Jones rides, are called twin-tipped snowboards. This means the front of the snowboard looks the same as the back of the snowboard. The snowboard is **symmetrical** so snowboarders can perform cool tricks in which they land in the fakie position. Snowboards are measured in centimeters. Most are about 160 cm (5.2 feet) long and 30 cm (1 foot) wide. Snowboarders secure their feet to the snowboard with a piece of **equipment** called bindings. Bindings are plastic straps that keep the board attached to the boots while snowboarders perform extreme tricks and ride on obstacles.

Kevin rides boards that are different lengths, one as short as 150 centimeters (5 feet), another as long as 160 centimeters (5.2 feet). Shorter snowboards allow riders more control. Longer snowboards can go faster.

Snowboarders often share the slopes with skiers. To enjoy the snowy slopes, skiers and snowboarders have to be respectful of one another. One thing that snowboarders and skiers have in common is that they just want to have a good time in the snow! Inset: Kevin performs a cool boardslide in competition.

Keeping It Safe on the Slopes

In order to have a good time and to stay safe, snowboarders use helmets. The U.S. Consumer Product Safety Commission (CPSC) advises all snowboarders to wear a helmet. The CPSC is a governmental group concerned with people's safety. In snowboarding, it is also important to dress in warm clothing. When you fall on snow, you get wet. If you are wet and it is cold outside, you can get sick. Kevin always wears a **waterproof** coat and pants, a hat, gloves, and warm clothing underneath. This keeps him from getting illnesses such as **hypothermia**. Kevin keeps warm on the slopes, and he also keeps his eyes safe with **goggles**.

Skiers and snowboarders often share the slopes. They do not always get along when they are on the mountain. Everybody must work to stay safe and be respectful!

21

In addition to being a great snowboarder, Kevin Jones is also an excellent fisherman. He spends time fly-fishing near his home in Bend, Oregon. Kevin even **qualified** to compete at the ESPN Great Outdoor Games in 2002. The Great Outdoor Games is a competition of events such as fishing and hunting. Kevin Jones spends most of his time snowboarding, but he competes in only a few snowboarding events per year.

Kevin loves to make snowboarding videos. He appears in these videos with other snowboarders, including Jussi Oksanen. Whether Kevin is shredding slopes in videos, spinning in midair in a competition, or winning an award, Kevin is always **inspiring** to his fans and fellow snowboarders.

Glossary

amazing (uh-MAYZ-ing) Excellent.

champions (CHAM-pee-unz) The best, or the winners.

championships (CHAM-pee-un-ships) Games held to decide the best, or the winner.

competition (kom-pih-TIH-shin) Game.

complex (kom-PLEKS) Very hard to do.

equipment (uh-KWIP-mint) All the supplies needed to do an activity.

extreme sport (ek-STREEM SPORT) A bold and uncommon sport, such as BMX, in-line skating, motocross, skateboarding, snowboarding, and wakeboarding.

goggles (GOG-elz) A kind of eyeglasses that fit close around your eyes.

half-pipes (HAF-pyps) Ramps that are shaped like a big *U*.

hypothermia (hy-poh-THUR-mee-uh) An illness in which body heat becomes too low.

inspiring (in-SPYR-ing) Filling others with feeling, wonder, or hope.

lightweight (LYT-wayt) Below normal weight.

materials (muh-TEER-ee-ulz) Fabrics or cloths.

medals (MEH-dulz) Small, round pieces of metal given as prizes.

obstacles (OB-stih-kulz) Objects that snowboarders use to perform tricks.

perform (per-FORM) To carry out, to do.

professional (pruh-FEH-shuh-nul) Paid for what he or she does.

qualified (KWAL-ih-fyd) Good enough to compete.

ramp (RAMP) A sloping platform.

skiers (SKEE-erz) People who use long, flat runners to ride over the snow.

sponsor (SPON-ser) To give gear and money to a sportsman or a sportswoman.

surfer (SERF-er) A person who uses a board to ride ocean waves.

symmetrical (sih-MEH-trih-kul) Describes an object that is the same on both sides.

waterproof (WAH-ter-proof) Not able to get wet.

Index

Web Sites

Due to the changing nature of Internet links, PowerKids Press has developed an online list of Web sites related to the subject of this book. This site is updated regularly. Please use this link to access the list: www.powerkidslinks.com/esb/jones/